ex

Author photo © Vicky Hindle

Steve O'Connor is a Mancunian living in West Yorkshire, where he teaches creative writing at colleges and libraries and runs bespoke distance learning courses. He devised and co-hosted Freed Up, which revolutionised the Manchester poetry scene, worked with Write Out Loud and transformed their Trafford-based poetry open mic night, and co-edited all three volumes of *Best of Manchester Poets*. He wants more people to write; it's his mission in life.

This is Steve's first full poetry collection. He hopes you like it.

"This collection betrays a controlled, at times resigned sensibility. They are a celebration of small moments as the means of having greater understanding, and a profound refinement from everyday emotions and thoughts. Sensitive but secure in outlook, these poems reveal a mature yet subtle vibrancy. Their economy of scale disguises their scope and concision."

> — *Robert Cochrane*
> *poet / The Bad Press*

"Like "the sting and throb of a new tattoo" these are painful and beautiful poems, worn on the sleeve and inked with care and precision. Unwrap their clingfilm, they will speak to the sunshine of rain."

> — *Tony Walsh AKA Longfella*
> *poet / educator*

"Steve O'Connor's words poetically brim 'n' blister with accomplished literary urgency. His scorching abilities to venture within and around his subjects, startling. On page or stage, this is work, living, breathing, a life-lived authenticity. From urban grits of scuffling city-scapes to fully-flown romances of human experience, Steve's poetry simply/complexly soars."

> — *Gerry Potter*
> *poet / playwright / director / actor*

"You can't beat Steve O'Connor for intelligent realism, for observation of humanity and quiet compassion. The gentle rhythms of his poetry only make clearer the fragility, that sense of being on the edge, of many people. I was going to say that he documents our times better than anyone, but what he actually does is to document life, existence and feeling, with intensity, insight, and flashes of panache. Impossible to read this without wanting to hug the man."

— *Cathy Thomas-Bryant*
poet / author / Puppywolf

"Here are heartfelt poems full of warmth, wit and imaginatively woven words. Lifelines of creativity and compassion for those of us who've taken more than our unfair share of beatings. Defiantly hopeful."

— *Dominic Berry*
poet / Saboteur Awards' Best Spoken Word Performer

"The love for people observed or well-known in their own complicated existences shines ... this is a celebration of the human existence in its smallest observations. Women in this collection have inner lives more vast and important than their outer appearance."

— *Anna Percy*
poet / Stirred Feminist Collective

Also by the author

freed up poet – love poems & cruel valentines [†]
Best of Manchester Poets, Vol. 1 (co-editor) [‡]
Best of Manchester Poets, Vol. 2 (co-editor) [‡]
Best of Manchester Poets, Vol. 3 (co-editor) [‡]

[†] Published by Freed Up [‡] Published by Puppywolf

STEVE O'CONNOR

e x t r a ñ o

To
Brett

Thanks!

Flapjack Press
www.flapjackpress.co.uk

Exploring the synergy between performance and the page

Steve O'Connor

Published in 2019 by Flapjack Press
Salford, Gtr Manchester
www.flapjackpress.co.uk

ISBN 978-1-9996707-6-4

Cover and author photos
copyright © Vicky Hindle

Cover design by Brink
www.paulneads.co.uk

Printed by Imprint Digital
Upton Pyne, Exeter, Devon
www.imprintdigital.com

City of
Literature

Dedicated to the memory of
Cyril Mellor.

Contents

A version of 'Study of a girl' was previously published in *Transparency* (Crocus, 2005).

'Electricity' was first published in *Best of Manchester Poets, Vol. 2* (Puppywolf, 2011).

'Birdsong' was first published in *I Know Where the City Has Wings* (Bad Language, 2010).

'Grace' and 'BMW' were first published in *Best of Manchester Poets, Vol. 1* (Puppywolf, 2010).

'Two lovers kiss' was first published in *Best of Manchester Poets, Vol. 3* (Puppywolf, 2013).

*Steve thanks Vicky Hindle, Emma Decent,
Geneviève L. Walsh, Kathy Walsh, John Darwin,
Gerry Potter, Robert Cochrane, Dionne Hood,
Cathy Thomas-Bryant, Keir Thomas-Bryant,
John G. Hall, Steve Rouse, Anna Percy,
Dominic Berry, Melanie Rees, Paul Neads,
absolutely anyone and everyone who made
Freed Up what it was, Bradford College,
YMCA Leeds, Bradford Libraries, Runcible
Spoon, Spoken Weird, the lovely people at
Wakefield College, Bradford City Library and
Ilkley Library creative writing learners,
and all of his friends and family.*

Foreword

Poetry: to a lot of us, it's the art form that fills the gaps in life that can't be filled with statistics and formulae. It takes still life paintings, photographs and nanosecond-long sound bites that we'd normally ignore and explores their importance. It deconstructs the ugly side of humanity that we're usually encouraged to block out with daft TV and useless trinkets, and celebrates love without resorting to inane chocolate box sentiment.

extraño is a collection that does all of the above exquisitely, but I'm painfully aware that the author would call me pretentious for leaving it there, so I'll also point out that there are some swear words and that it's probably not a suitable gift for your nan.

Many of you will know Steve O'Connor as an unforgettable performer of poignant poetry, and his visceral, earth-shaking Mancunian voice is present throughout this collection, but he's never been a one-man band in terms of his subject matter. He's a writer who speaks for the forgotten, unknown and underrated souls among us. The blink-and-you'll-miss-them lovers, loners, workers, worriers and warriors in Steve's poems will truly come to life when you read this collection.

Geneviève L. Walsh
Spoken Word Artist

extraño

Freed up

Exiled scholars and garret wallahs
Braying, wailing against the dollar
Frantic for the next epiphany
Scrambling for that hit of clarity
Have realised where it doesn't lurk
It's not in your cubicle at work
In magazines at supermarkets
Or the daytime TV chat show topic
It's always been here – like a clue
Found by dirty-faced kids wagging school
Sticking like shit to new shoes
Its truth as true as a new bruise
It's world-changing, cruel and kind
To the sternest of buttoned-down thinking minds
It questions function, it rejects style
Makes you take the deepest breath then smile
Utterly revolutionises
And takes all theories considered wise
Scrutinises them until they're husks
Sees if shoots grow from the dust
And nurtures those fresh ideas
And it's simply this
All the freaks, the marginalised, the queer
Know that it's a futile pursuit
But revel in its beauty
Rail and wind like cyclones
Dance like scuttling bugs found beneath stones
And dare to because you won't
But still refuse to be called heroic
They are the challengers of the unknown
The artists, the freed-up poets.

The message

Your message arrived today;
A potent communiqué.
It lay on the doormat,
Slim, white envelope fat with intent,
Words to relay.

I stared and stared at it
For about twenty minutes.
Your sender's address scrawl
Clawed my thoughts, snuffed them out.
Left one lit.

I fancied you frowning
In your ink-smeared dressing gown.
Tear-soaked wrists wrangled, flicked
Your message down. A misplaced kiss.
Word gets around.

But inside? A poem.
Bones reassembled as light,
I cried for love reignited
And the urgency of three words sown –
"Please come home."

Study of a girl

Suggested by Study of a Girl, *a sketch by Gwen John.*

You look lonely and content,
sitting amid the aftermath
of a storm of mindful yearning.

Fascinated by this new ruin,
choice provides you things
to rebuild, the rest to scatter.

Your lips remain pursed,
eyes accusing, a rock in your hand,
a blushing cheek spared by your hood.

Our love once coursed through
shared veins. Now you sit
statue still, the bloodied rock
in your hands.

Return

His arms have grown too long
from battering away thoughts
prior to his return.
Puts down his bow.
Picks up his bag.
Hails cabs instead of friend or foe
and hopes summer lightning renders
memory intangible.
Celebrates the trivial with popping corks,
hoops and snares.
Creates the diaphanous to detract from the scar
that runs through him.
Lugs a jaded trunk, drowns
in the ordinary.
Last curses spat at cruel thoughts
whose snide promises manifest
like an incomplete jigsaw.
A final lust to cut the throat of a god,
punch victoriously through the fabric,
leave a wordless shadow, nothing more.

Penguin woman

Penguin woman walks imaginary hills
Takes two steps then stops and checks her pockets
Hands like spatulas slowly scooping nothing
She shrugs shoulders down into a burdened breath

Tongue clucking, looking down the road
She shifts her weight like a stood-up date, sighing
Her make-up's three days old; her shoes are scuffed and flat
Feet slap like paddles up the cruel angled cobbles

At the entrance to the park she stops again
Turns hopeful as if somebody's called her name
Turns back to where a young girl sometimes plays
Though not today

Penguin woman walks down well-remembered paths
Where shaded cigarettes were shared and smoked discreetly
Swollen flesh, stolen kisses and nasty rashes
When laughter sang of adventure and not scorn.

How queer

A pretty face was a curse for the boy
A gentle nature too
But bravery and honesty
bring out the worst in fools
Their punches and their kicks
No more than proof of false decree
    Still, as sorry as I felt
    I was glad it wasn't me

We'd walk home from school together
And you'd always make me laugh
Singing the latest by Madonna
Being juvenile and daft
Spinning yarns out of cruel wit
Entwining tales of just revenge
    But I was fearful to admit
    That I would ever call you 'friend'

You'd endure the shouts of 'beast'
You'd ignore their spiteful sneers
Defiant silence to their violence
Never showing any tears
Quiet courage was your weapon
Humanity in open hand
    And though you had my admiration
    I didn't understand

We lost touch with each other
And a festering fable grew
Of a young man who does things
In a way that's most taboo

I could not figure out
Why your name stirred up such blood
    Surely one has to know the bad
    To appreciate the good?

Rumour fades like reputation
Of a gossip's false renown
I found out you'd met a nice bloke
Naturally, you settled down
Discovered joy amid the torment
A pleasant life for you instead
    I was glad for your successes
    Then I blinked – you were dead

I'll never know why you suffered
So quietly at length
I won't get to say how much
I admire you for your strength
Twenty-one years old is death
At far too cheap a price
    And regret instead of friendship
    Will never suffice.

Christic of St. John of the Cross

Suggested by Christ of Saint John of the Cross, *a painting by Salvador Dalí.*

Dalí's helicopter blades twirl
Swish like upturned moustache tips
Slash like a Stanley knife blade
Across the surface of Christ's shadow
Clouds gather in mute observance
Subbuteo fishermen stand caught
By the coarse sheet metal lake
Girded by flaccid mounds
Longing to belong to Gala's curves.

Milieu

Suggested by Veiled Eiffel Tower, *a photograph by Lee Miller.*

Parisians fall onto streets
shaking sleep from their heads,
final morsels of dreams of a structure
that can't have existed;
a half-glimpsed mirage standing at the corner,
brooding like an overseer,
desperate to remain unforgotten.
Sleet falls screening an out-of-vogue subject
and no more photos are taken.

Afternoons in winter

Afternoons in winter
Etch a trail in greasy formica
Smear the points of a compass scrawl
Carly luvs…?
A scoured name

Afternoons in winter
Windows steam like clogged-up lungs
Minutes distend in sips of tea
Excited children
And Wi-Fi

Afternoons in winter
The draught of clatter and chatter
Yesterday's free papers
Damp dog-walkers
With full pockets.

Communication

In an airport lounge
language flits between a mother
and a son.

"When will it come?" the son asks.
The bud of his mother's mouth folds.

Electricity

Today the sun defies the rain
Shines on the street, cuts through
The morning like an overheard
Five a.m. whistle or the scent
And ghost-buzz of post-storm air
Reigns in the silence, spreads it over
The flimsy skin of these early hours
Yearns to stretch, bend its blank rays,
Dazzle into ears all cut-throat and noiseless
Callous sunrise rejects gravity and blazes and blazes
Then sputters as it sparkles
Flickers like jewels hidden beneath beetle wings
And sinks into the loudest shadow.

Light bends

Can you hear that rumbling?
Four in the morning and the boiler's clearing its throat
Pipes tap-tapping, rapping on old joists
Laddered padding long since worn
Round metal that crosses buried crosses
Beneath well-weathered floorboards

Daylight's been out all night
And now rattles round the window
Stretches itself around the curtains
A vampire victim of the night bus
Stumbling from the electric kick
And jangle noise of an ill-driven milk float

First light wants in, begging
And will sing its brightness through tight-shut eyelids
Hoodwink, hook and force you to look
At the room's mute colours waking up
A bedside book, a half-empty cup
And the shadow of a full ashtray

Daybreak bends its rays
Prises open a dusty day
Greedy as a grave-robber at the mouth of a tomb
Crooked beams stir creaking bones
The night's now stolen – morning owns
All that it covets, all that it exhumes.

Birdsong

Traffic hums like an approving parent
Captivated by other pursuits
Oblivious to the sport of birds
Flitting between branches and singing
The history of the trees
Each high whistle a story of blossom falling
Sweet scented spring rain
Or a season's stray eyelash brushed away
By warmer days

Beneath a hot swell of scrutiny
The bark creaks and a feast gushes
From the gash – a Dionysian pantry
Of bugs, beasts and other treats
To fill the beaks and stomachs
Of hungry hatchlings
Vomit soup nurtures those who cling
To the nest – a famished chorus
A greedy, needy nursery

And the low notes tell a tale of darker days
Invaders fought until blood fell from the sky
Gives warning of territory
And of a time a grimalkin climbed the tree
Spitefully slashing and dashing the youngest
To the unforgiving concrete
White spatters around the roots
Amassed like years of paint
Spilled carelessly

In each bird's song there is a legend
That transforms to symphony. It dips and rises
Like a descent of hollow-boned bodies
Hearts fluttering in air pockets
This chaotic genealogy –
Recurrent origins that dare to grow from shoots
Exposed to nature's cruelty
Holds fast to the footpath
And will one day silence the motorway.

Perfect city

Its mornings are washed in post-storm sunlight, burnishing slate roofs on sleepy-eyed homes, casting shadows on streets dusted down with a baked bread scent.

Its song is the creak and clunk of a front door that fills the world and shakes the sunrise from its slumber; each dawn a melody and rhythm for footfall to fathom.

Its expression is found beneath the weathered surface of stone, steel and spray; an answer half-heard, ever changing in prospect, or the mood of a new arrival.

Its humour burbles like the eager grumble of an engine ticking over, where impatient seconds open up as chasms making the day's promise seem unreachable.

Its journey carries vessels along paths that defy compass readings to places that threaten opportunity and deliver choices. Such sustenance can feed and poison.

Its work is methodical and to the point, pausing only for tea and chitchat about biscuits; a mannered preamble to conversation concerning holidays not yet taken.

Its talk is fuelled by mischief, like the wicked joy of a child discovering swear-words, or a playful flirtation between colleagues that's recognised but never acted upon.

Its dusk shimmers and allows everything to fall from its grasp, save for a few precious remnants; the warming satisfaction that comes from time filled with significance.

Its roads pulse with traffic, viewpoints in transit keen for fresh discoveries, hot rumour of alliances, forsaken appointments and laughter that conceals teeth-gritted envy.

Its care responds to the sound of the wine glass smashing against the wall of the over-priced flat. It's the arm around the shoulder under the railway arch where tears fall.

Its noise ricochets between buildings and down alleyways like the fade-out on a much-loved refrain, 'til all that's discernible is an affectionate whisper of farewell.

Its nights give shelter and tranquillity to the lucky who have avoided its inevitable rain, where heavy-eyed thoughts drift and cloud the mind into dreams of a perfect city.

What is it and what could it be?

In the final drawer
On the morning of the clearance
Long undisturbed by mysteries
Hovering over soapboxes and items rearranged
A few now discovered things
All solid and haphazard
Like fingers pointing towards crevices
Away from discovery
Shaped and separate objects
With undisclosed stories
Looking for repurpose or conversation
Maybe even the happiest connection
Beauty – whatever that means.

Grace

Grace can think in bullet-time
Throw a thought around and make you duck
Before it hits you
Beats up stuff until it works
Has been known to go berserk
Makes mirrors flinch and pinch themselves
Awake in her reflection
Gives water an erection
And with one swing of her hips
Shadow-bound spiders fall to their knees and worship

Grace is smooth and intense
White chocolate-dipped honeycomb out of the freezer
Turns burns to ice-cold showers
And knows the difference between heat and warmth
Will not explain what you already know
So don't ask
She'll tease out your story
She's read every book on life-drawing
Draws breath that tastes of red wine kisses
And colours not yet invented

Grace is daft
Has the kind of laugh found at funfairs
Only ever uses two swear words
Uses both to power her ray-gun
Bubblegum-pop laser beams
Knickers ride up the bum of this anime ASBO angel
High-kicking her own battle of the planets
Never plans – but can read tea leaves
Gets the future – so she doesn't have to
Will one day speak Japanese – maybe

Grace wrote the book
On what it means to touch and be touched
And how to cut the bullshit
Totally uninhibited in her charm
Disarms you with a glance
Can't dance, can't sing – wrote a song about it
For her book
Cooks in the bedroom, fucks in the kitchen
So much more than a bewitching tease
One day she'll teach me Japanese.

Stud

You're fumblings at fifteen
Leather jacket cool
Bedroom walls painted black
And marijuana flapjacks

You're shuffling to 'Love Cats'
In sweaty-walled nightclubs
The love that makes loins ache
My mate's favourite piss-take

Hasty but no mistake
Or blue turning tattoo
Bigots rush to call queer
You've always had my ear

You're the snarl and the sneer
For your daddy's princess
"Stay away from that boy"
Thirty years you've annoyed

The deserve-to-be-annoyed
You're all the gold I own
Punctured through my skin
You're never ever leaving.

Youth

This world deserves more than I can give
All I have are pockets full of pavement cracks
Ideas bubble-wrapped, tightly fit to pop
And tiny monsters lurking waiting for a full stop
When the morning alarm sounds
You'll find me scuttling beneath duvet
Winding guide ropes around the sun
Manifesting a fractured horizon
Willing the day to come undone
Swill, spill and overflow
Deny all I think I know
For all that's fit for this day
An eye cast over the top of the duvet
Worrying, foppish and feeble words that say
The best kind of love is longing and always unrequited
Why else would I feel so hungry?
Why else would I feel so slighted?

The funfair

Bodies spin, stomachs churning
Wurlitzing like teenage yearning
Shrieks whip up a sugar-snap
Ozone crack cherry-pink beehive hairdo
For tonight the scrubland is suited and booted
Embraces the fair – holds tight
As snug as a razor-bladed lapel

That flush in your cheek is a fighting chance
The iron in your blood – the weekend
Squeezing through overcrowded veins
Jostling for that single release
A victory where metal meets metal
In a grasp that's as far from tender
As lips are from a steel toe-cap kiss

The funfair has hit the town
So all the lads cruise down
Looking smart and fit
Don't they all look fucking cool?
Don't they all look up for it?

And the girls seek a similar sort
Of cruelty to their sport
But with a focus that's far straighter
Victims get what they deserve
Then a finger's worth of fit lad later

The preening and the glamour
Hands unseen and clamour
Of voices dragging laughter across the surface of machines
    that struggle against the inevitable rust

This many people can only mean
Pleasure at its most hostile

Like the last minute of a summer's evening
That ends with a wasp's sting
The prize that decorates the drain
With all the suffocated goldfish
Triumphs ring as hollow as a test your strength bell
When you say – *Scream if you want to go faster*
You mean – *Scream. I won't tell.*

The reception

Baby screams over the chorus
Causes the record to jump
Guests shuffle round the sticky patch
Eyeing it cautiously
Treating it suspiciously
Evidence of the killjoy attendee
And the rudest of interruptions
Somewhere in another room
Away from family and witnesses
A new bride cries the bitterest tears
Poetic vows, laughter at rice thrown
But this is the memory that'll persist
Mascara stains a once-worn dress's wrists
Where eyes are wiped and wiped again
And bridesmaids sigh at chances missed
And pray it never happens to them
In a corner, by the bar
Superficial words are slung like drunken punches
Or a best man's boasts
Glasses raised in toast lie smashed
A mother contemplates
Taking her hat back to the shop
The dancing doesn't stop
The DJ tries a joke
The groom fades to another shade of grey
Gagging for a smoke
One of many sacrifices centred round today
Father and father-in-law over a pint agree
They have wasted their money
And give it six months at best

In an hour hostilities will cease
But no-one will forget
The girl who couldn't forever hold her peace
The uninvited guest.

Dirty weekend

Chipped china cup half washed up
Rests in her hands
Forty-a-day smoker stains
Tepid tea sloshes down the drain
Sodden biscuit crumb remains
Glistening like fools' gold
She never dreamt she'd be this old
And have to start again
Without her man
Wedding vows aren't worth a damn
I do's give way to the big I am
Voices raised, front doors slammed
And the cruelty of a husband and a friend
Leaves her the victim of a dirty weekend

School run planned, lies on demand
It's now all in her hands
A lead weight around a necessary task
She'll tut-tut, act dismissive
To childish questions asked
Blow the neighbours kisses
Unpack the weekly shopping
And pray that her mask doesn't slip
Rumour gives way to gossip
She knows supermarket shelves are stacked
With sordid stories of divorces
And marriages ransacked
So she'll smile and continue to pretend
There's no such thing as a dirty weekend

She's alone, she understands
The blood is on his hands
The rest of him "another woman's stink"
It's bedtime, loves
She swallows pills, she has a drink
It's over in the time it takes to blink
And further falsehoods will prevail
Concealing weakness and betrayal
And all will be observed by younger eyes
They'll come to learn the truth, they'll despise
When there's no answer to the simple question *Why?*
That isn't stupid, spineless, feeble, sick, blithe
And no amount of back-pedalling will mend
The consequences of a dirty weekend.

BMW

Straight man turns forty in a paper party hat
Above board, mod-shirted
Razor-cut hair square to his accurate collar
Follows pub politics for more than kicks
Smears his words with casual bigotry
And has never kissed his son
Knows what the back of his hand is for
And has never kissed his son
Works diligently for his holidays
Can detail a day-by-day scam
Proper good with engines
"Like every man should be"
Will see you right for your MOT
And your wife
Calculates his smile
Brims with guile
Wouldn't mind a night in Styal Women's Prison
Wears derision like a fat man wears Speedos
And wears Speedos in all his sun-kissed photos
Sunburned onto your retina
Talks tenderly of his Angelina
The multi-coloured Ford Cortina
He drove at seventeen
Leather jacketed, pay-packeted cruiser
Lean leans to lean over and topples with girth
Inevitable with age
As sure as earth scatters across coffin lids
His kids will never go without
Won't learn from what it means to have nowt
And treasure those memories
Three times away to parts unknown each year

Fears queers
Likes bikes
And time apart from the wife
Seems to live a life of rosy-cheeked
Strictly white male bonding
And falling on the sword
And other such pursuits manly men get up to
When they're bored.

The joke that leaves a sour aftertaste

Ever present in the pub
Like a Toby Jug gathering dust
He sits beneath His name
In His corner and judges
A pissed-up His Honour
A slurrer of uncivil words
Waits with ruddy face
And a case to put forward
Says something earnest
As he grabs your elbow
Would like to get to know you well
Skips about like the record
On the too-used, not demanded jukebox
Popular – like chickenpox
Asks if you don't mind racist jokes
Secretly wouldn't mind changing
The pub's name to
The Rubicon Crossed
All that it signifies in his eyes
Eyes you sipping Diet Coke and wonders
If this is the first of the evening's blunders
Dreams of absconding with the till
And Old Gill's bristols
(She pulled a mean pint until that unfortunate fight
With breast cancer)
Still dreams
Still waits until the bell is rung
Dreams of what he'll do once the bell is rung.

Holocaust deniers

Come out from under the pond scum
Come down from out of the trees
Evolution's a revolution that will set your anger at ease
Evidence of inbreeding is all you'll find in purity
So come out from under the pond scum
Come down from out of the trees

Join us by our fire (an ancient discovery)
Learn from other cultures
Extend your vocabulary
Cast aside your hatred and dangerous bigotry
Come out from under the pond scum
Come down from out of the trees

I'm not saying that you're stupid
After all you're just like me
Except I fail to see the sense in rewriting history
Whose cruelty has provoked such crass insensitivity?
Come out from under the pond scum
Come down from out of the trees

Still, your bestial attacks increase in their ferocity
We look to the past and label you an old monstrosity
You take pride in that and glory in each of your atrocities
The symbols you worship? Nothing but rank animosity

You shout and you shout and you continue to devolve
Hateful words, loathsome actions which can never be absolved
You smile like you're winning if your children are involved
I call that proof that you don't want to evolve

Your recurring psychopaths with their empty theories
A vacant and tiresome narrative that spits
Come out from under the pond scum
Come down from out of the trees
Who deserves the right to 'discuss'?
Who deserves Auschwitz?

Play war

Lie down, close your eyes, count to ten
Before the call to rise comes again
Listen for the rattle; the machine gun's cackle
Suffer the slaughter of men

Ascend into view like the sun
That shines upon life come undone
Tell us a tale that helps war prevail
Heroism – a yarn to be spun

Bound with fire in your stride
Each battle is fuel for your pride
All today's glories are tomorrow's old stories
Written in blood and tears dried

Honour the oath that you swore
Never question the types who keep score
Overlook all those dead. It was Hitler who said
"But that's what the young men are there for"

Dash to that final Amen
With the vigour of your fallen friends
The untrustworthy weep whilst their champions sleep
So lie down, close your eyes, count to ten.

The risk not taken

One might think it easy
After smiles and cordial words
Talk that lingers – hopeful
Like daylight clings to summer evenings

But I falter like a coward
Dare not to brave your face
Dissidence dissuades me
From such tremulous impulses

Should I risk your glance?
Be subject to your scrutiny?
Could I ask and withstand
The weight of your decision?

I hold coyness in contempt
As much as coyness holds me back
I curse reserve's restraints
And clasp at nervous words

You suggest a drink sometime
And I try to not look shocked
Flustering responses dress up
Dithering and pithy

Time slips a slight frown
Between eyes that seek an answer
Hesitance prises free
Reasons as obstacles

Your shrug and 'See you soon'
Seems wrapped in guarantee
We raise our hands as if to touch
Then resign ourselves to waving

And this summer afternoon
Pales to a scant degree
Assurances, as such,
Are a danger I'll risk braving.

Clouds at sunset

Footprints left in wet sand
Dance a path towards a red horizon
Where the sky hangs like fresh laundry
And flutters with a scent
Of clouds at sunset

We play kiss-chase with the tide
Stand defiant at the shore
Shouting demands at invisible ships
Refunds of deposits on message-less bottles
And rude words to shame sailors

This day's end will not fall
It rises like sunburn
Like laughter that swells
From the belly to the throat
And blushes clouds at sunset

We are vandals breaking up the evening
Leaving nothing but splinters
And a threat of first light
Your smile is the catalyst
The graceful spark that resists the gloaming

I offer my open hand to the flame
I volunteer my life and will to this moment
This perfect undertow must transgress
Reach skyward and snatch back
Clouds at sunset

Hold them fast in an embrace
That sustains like the ocean's roar
The chaos music of gull-song
Have our trail remain a joyous stumbling minuet
To the noise of clouds at sunset.

Two lovers kiss

Two lovers kiss
Taj Mahaling the bus station
Skinny-tied tight lips smacking
Buffering cheekbones sharper than pointed brogues

They pause, compose a moment that ticks
Like twin tongues against lip-rims
Then dive in again
Fresh and clean in their dirtiest clothes

Who knows what they're waiting for?
Who cares?

Stretch the seconds like spittle strands
Burn schedules, snap axles
Contort the night with molten metal mouths
Fire defiance at disapproving barriers

Grasp the blaze's threads and unwind it
Down, down. Reveal its primal spark
Caress and fasten it between
And then kiss.

Feasting

A final word uttered
And I can taste its gritty residue
Along the back of my teeth;
Sweet sand washed to my tongue's gangplank,
Slowly diving into my stomach,
Leaving a feast of hunger
For when you're gone.

Looking for an easy kill,
You have made soup from my bones and fed me.
Graced my lips with a now ceaseless thirst for you.
Distance is starvation,
So, remain and sate every moment.
Let each draught hang with your redolence,
Each gelid gust drown in your warmth.

You stir and kiss me.
Hot mixed stale wine and saliva
Assault my palate, triggering memory
Where tastes lie waiting to be shocked.
Yet, we have consumed that which was tempered,
Immodest in our gluttony,
Blithe in each other's juices.

Do not leave. Scraps alone will not sustain us
And emptiness is nothing
If not a lesser-craved discovery.
Stay. I'll swallow your words,
Wash them down with unforeseen voracity,
Save for that final choking utterance:
Your farewell.

Knock-back

And you lie there in the gloom
Contemplating how to forsake
Love's dream once thought engulfed
Now dry, shaken and awake

I'm a just-revived drowned man
Bones heavy with thirst's weight
A vessel that cannot hold
Soaked but at the same time drained

I drag myself from your room
More slaughtered and less slaked
Drinking in darkness's draught
As naked as daybreak

We have swallowed all our sourness
As much as both of us could take
A medicine as tart as tears
To cure regret and mistakes.

BASTARDS

There are people who take delight in your failure
There are those who actively despise your success
Vehemently compartmentalise their hatred
Thrust the minutes down your life's throat
They don't know every second in your arms is a victory
Each moment – an archer's symbol of splendid defiance
They'll never understand. They couldn't understand
Because… they are bastards
Leeching everything from us but our breath
And our love

Some individuals savour the distasteful
Spit out venom with an ungodly relish
Dress-up their ill-mannered excreta as manna
And claim breeding whilst pulling at the push door
They can't see how your smile makes me feel light-headed
Switches a billion balloons with my brain
How could they comprehend?
It's a tricky twig to grasp
And what's more… they're bastards
Slowly hollowing us out and leaving
A few sparks

And they can try to tamp us down
Restrict us
Construct a vessel of inflictions
But once that powder keg's built
It'll only ever do one thing

The rabble like to swarm, grab and molest you
Les Tricoteuses fabricating the uninformed
Cry out "horror" with hands hidden in their pockets

They deride you. They really need you to like them
They don't get how your wit can disintegrate a bastard
And when your lips part you can split apart a bastard
A glare from your eyes can atomise a bastard
Run and hide! Run and hide, *all* bastards!
We wield our love like sharpened scimitars
We ride maddened chargers, eyes fixed and deep-red
We'll bring hooves down on the head of every bastard
And refuse them the gift of mourning when they're dead.

Love kisses goodbye

Your love runs
Through my memories
Like treacle

Your kisses linger
Hold my lips
Refuse to let go

Your goodbye still hurts
Burns hot like an August sun –
Turns skin to syrup.

Bring me...

Curtains to shut out the light
The last *t* from my love's good night
Pillows for a leaden head
The oblivion from recurrent zeds
A duvet over which to peep
And bring me one more hour of sleep!

Carrot girl

Carrot girl loved carving carrots
Didn't know when to stop
She carved parrots out of carrots
Made desert islands from the tops
Added a little deckchair
A beach hut and public loo
Sanitation, irrigation
The odd hotel or two
An orange crunchy supermarket
Not Waitrose, but a Spar
Carrot theme pubs and nightclubs
Roads to drive your carrot car
And loads of carrot people came
Trashed the nice carroty place
'Til it no longer seemed the same
Our girl had the saddest face
She was despondent, really un-orange
Very blue indeed
But all of that would change
On the day she met her Swede.

People like us

Suggested by 'People Like Us', a poem by Jackie Hagan.

We don't see in black and white
Wear mannered movie star faces
Or speak in transatlantic clipped tones

We cut the cord on mobile phones
Spin down dancefloor crevices
Swing the moon across the night

Avoid the threat of morning
Defiant duvet, creative swearing
And a mouthful of yawning

When we're told to "get a job"
We repel such malignant incantations
By cultivating bonsai limps

Camp and rough and daft
Unnerving laughter at the back of the bus
Fumbling in crisp packets

Like the dirty bastards we are
Stale-breathed death worshippers
Rain-spattered sloppy kissers

We know all of your forgotten secrets
And have turned them into poems
Swallowed that bottle's last pill

And if you're truly like us
Then your first name must be Our
Pronounced "are", rhymes with "love"

And if you're truly like us
Then your throat bears the scars
Of your tears

All the hidden colours
The skinned knee at six
The broken heart at seventeen

We have them
We've kept them.

Charlotte works at Poundland

Morning drivers of angry taxis
Heave head-long across the ground
Dreams of nonstop Friday nights
Pristine cabs, abandoned purses

Ungracious monotony
Is all that Monday offers
Gritty rain on paving stones
Dull rays cast on bus stops

Charlotte, cool in cagoule
Stands staring at the tarmac
Willing the day to ignite
Catch and burn away the hours

Elastic tight snap slap right
Into work behind the till
Charlotte's got a shift to kill
Charlotte works at Poundland

She's Clara Bow in polyester
Ambitions unfathomed
She's given up, struggled back to life
Secrets at a discount

She's polo-shirt-noosed
Let loose with today's prices
Scoots around the edge of things
Pockets plastic earrings

Recognises customers
Who know the history of the shelves
More than she ever will
Won't look them in the eye

Today she'll watch the bastard clock
Defy each second's cursed tick
Time might be a suicide
But this girl? She has plans

A slow stroll to and from the kettle
Lunch stretched to the point of snapping
Laughter at the weekly meeting
A sudden blood rush to her cheeks

Yawning at next week's promotions
Stock creeping past expiry moved
Spillages on aisle two
The sting and throb of a new tattoo

Her final stretch distends, inflates
Bloats and blots out barcode bleeps
She feels life rattling in her teeth
She aches to scream the world away

At five past six she's stood outside
The taxi arrives with the rain
Her cagoule's plastered to her skin
Her uniform is in the bin

A name scored on tissue thin
Is as much branded on her brain
She gives the driver an address
Says it once and then again

They'll never know she's met a girl
They won't guess why she's run away
Yes, Charlotte worked at Poundland
But today was her last day.

Party to it

Slump on the stairs with me
Lie here and talk of all we hate
As I do my best James Dean
Red-label Thunderbird sedated
Eyes squint, upturned collar
Desires and designs on you
As your mates dance on the sofa
Because your folks are in Corfu

Bass kicks like a pissed-up ninja
And something in the kitchen crashes
You say something vodka-breathed
Forceful though your false eyelashes
Speak of recent tears
Your hands gesture like you couldn't care
Betrayal in your sneer
A whiff of vomit in your hair

And words that should embarrass
Hang between beats as the music breaks
This night has turned to trespass
Where noise and booze drowns out the ache
That makes me shake for you
I've felt like this since I was ten
Could you feel the same way too?
Will we ever be this alive again?

We turn and run upstairs
Past a crying girl, a carpet stain
And what was once a wicker chair
To your parents' bathroom

Where you slide the chain across the door
Then fall with me into the bath
Away from the party's roar
We lie and laugh and laugh and laugh.

You

There's nothing wrong with you
Not fitting in is a good thing
No meaningless chit-chat about banal television
Or labels you're not wearing
You're interesting
Your talk's stimulating
You've read books thick as doorsteps
And you know who'd win
In a fight between Robocop and Judge Dredd

There's nothing wrong with you
You prefer living to brain-death
You've not been abroad for ages, if ever
And that's really quite admirable
You can be tough to be with
Your laugh's pleasant and filthy
You're a credible liar and won't apologise
For the racists in your family

And all the people who think you're weird
Well, they're right
But those bores who crave being the centre of attention
Have all the charm of pubic lice

There's nothing wrong with you
You turn skint into sexy
The designer gear goes well with the stuff
From B&M Bargains
You're a pretty good kisser
You're a terrible dancer
You've one qualification
GCSE Dance
And you copied the answers

There's nothing wrong with you
Your face should be that shape
You don't get to have thoughts as dirty as yours
Without some sort of impact
You can be devil and angel
You know quotes from The Bible
You're saving them all
For that day when you go
Full-blown homicidal

And all of those who consider themselves
Community moral pillars
Should know that those who're picked last for team sports
Become geniuses (or serial killers)

But what's written in notes
Documented in surgeries
Is nothing more than ill-conceived judgements
Scribbled in margins
Because you are heroic
And repel all attackers
Who fill you and will you with pills
'Til you trill like a human maraca

There's nothing wrong with you
You draw breath and you give love
Your words can save lives
And your arse can turn dull Sunday afternoons sticky
You cry like you laugh
But what you're not hearing
Is there's nothing wrong with you
Nothing at all
Not fitting in is a good thing.

Our hero

When the book was closed
The adventure put away
Our hero gave a sigh

Stretched his creaking bones
Rested his feet of clay
When the book was closed

To the sound of good night groans
And night snuffing out day
Our hero gave a sigh

Sleep fell like temple stones
Into dreams where victors play
When the book was closed

Mummies thwarted, pharaohs' thrones
Fall to the thud of hitting hay
Our hero gave a sigh

And tales tiredness condones
Were put aside, were held at bay
When the book was closed
Our hero gave a sigh.

Find us

Find us between cups of tea
And butties doorstep thick
Visits to beloved friends
Where clock hands never stick
Sloshing down the sweet and hot
Being buttered-up like bread
Laughing at old jokes
Suggesting new punchlines instead

Find us red-leading pylons
Sitting at drab workstations
Manning drills to pay the bills
Dreaming of vacation
In air-conditioned offices
Or sweating in the sun
Arriving home each evening
With a sense of job well done

Find us worshipping deities
Prayer and tears and smiles
Kneeling with an open heart
Or dancing in the aisles
Striving to improve ourselves
Seeking answers within
Blissful in epiphanies
Or feeling that there's nothing

Find us in old photographs
Of lovers now departed
Where snap-shot smiles could not predict
Such breadth of grief uncharted

Wrapped in tender memory
To dull the sense of loss
Tokens of treasured moments
That love has spread across

Find us drawing our last breath
Find us breathing our first
Then being held to mother's breast
Should it be flesh or earth
Find us on screens, in books, in dreams
Ridiculous! Profound
We're magnificent
We're *people*
We're here
And we abound!